The Ultimate Power XL Air Fryer Grill Cookbook For Beginners

Beginners Guide To Impress Your Friends With Mouth-Watering Roasts, Bake, And Meals With The Power XL Air Fryer Grill

Nancy Cooke

Copyright - 2021 - All rights reserved.

The content contained within this book may not be reproduced, duplicated or transmitted without direct written permission from the author or the publisher.

Under no circumstances will any blame or legal responsibility be held against the publisher, or author, for any damages, reparation, or monetary loss due to the information contained within this book. Either directly or indirectly.

Legal Notice:

This book is copyright protected. This book is only for personal use. You cannot amend, distribute, sell, use, quote or paraphrase any part, or the content within this book, without the consent of the author or publisher.

Disclaimer Notice:

Please note the information contained within this document is for educational and entertainment purposes only. All effort has been executed to present accurate, up to date, and reliable, complete information. No warranties of any kind are declared or implied. Readers acknowledge that the author is not engaging in the rendering of legal, financial, medical or professional advice. The content within this book has been derived from various sources. Please consult a licensed professional before attempting any techniques outlined in this book.

By reading this document, the reader agrees that under no circumstances is the author responsible for any losses, direct or indirect, which are incurred as a result of the use of information contained within this document, including, but not limited to, - errors, omissions, or inaccuracies.

TABLE OF CONTENTS

INTRODUCTION 10

BREAKFAST 12

1. Tasty Coconut Almond Donuts 13

2. Zucchini Strawberry Cheesy Casserole 15

3. Lemon Chili Buttery Baked Pumpkin 17

4. Cabbage Hash Brown with Spinach and Bacon 19

5. Coconut Sandwich with Tomato and Avocado 21

MAINS: BEEF 24

1. Easy Beef Roast 25

2. Beef Sirloin Roast 26

3. Air Fried Grilled Steak 28

MAINS: SEAFOOD 30

1. Lemon-Pepper Tilapia Fillets 31

2. Blackened Shrimp with Lemon Juice 33

3. Fried Catfish with Fish Fry 35

4. Pecan-Crusted Catfish Fillets 36

5. Fish Fillets with Parmesan Cheese 38

6. Air-Fried Sardines 40

MAINS: VEGETABLES 42

1. Curried Eggplant Slices 43

2. Healthy Green Beans 44

MAINS: POULTRY ... 46
1. Spicy Air-Crisped Chicken and Potatoes ... 47
2. Buttermilk Fried Chicken ... 50
3. Korean Chicken Wings ... 52
4. Paprika Chicken Wings ... 55

MAINS: PORK ... 58
1. Spiced Pork Shoulder ... 59
2. Seasoned Pork Tenderloin ... 61
3. Garlicky Pork Tenderloin ... 63

SNACKS ... 66
1. Personal Mozzarella Pizza Crust ... 67
2. Garlic Cheese Bread ... 69
3. Crustless Three-Meat Pizza ... 70
4. Bacon-Wrapped Brie ... 71
5. Smoky BBQ Roasted Almonds ... 73

SIDES ... 76
1. Low-Calorie Beets Dish ... 77
2. Broccoli and Parmesan Dish ... 79
3. Bacon and Asparagus Spears ... 80
4. Healthy Low Carb Fish Nugget ... 82
5. Fried Up Pumpkin Seeds ... 83
6. Decisive Tiger Shrimp Platter ... 85

DESSERT 88
1. Vegan Donuts 89
2. Cinnamon Rice with Coconut 90
3. Pineapple and Apricots 91
4. Air-Fried Smores 92
5. Banana Smores 94
6. Cherry Pie 96
CONCLUSION 98

INTRODUCTION

Congratulations on purchasing my cookbook.

I designed these recipes to be able to prepare them thanks to the use of an indispensable tool in today's kitchen. I'm talking about the Power XL air fryer.

What can you cook with this appliance? The answer is simple, everything you want.

Where can you find ideas for cooking amazing dishes? Again the answer is simple, you will find inspiration in this cookbook!

I am sure that the recipes that I will propose to you shortly will please you very much and above all, with the minimum effort to prepare them, they will conquer your palate and that of your friends.

Enjoy your meal!

BREAKFAST

1. Tasty Coconut Almond Donuts

Preparation Time: 5 Minutes
Cooking Time: 25 Minutes
Servings: 4

Ingredients:

- 2 tablespoons almond flour
- 1-tablespoon coconut flour
- ½ tablespoon psyllium husk
- ½ teaspoon xanthan gum
- ½ cup unsweetened almond milk
- 2 tablespoons coconut oil
- A pinch of salt
- 2 eggs
- 1-tablespoon extra-virgin olive oil

Directions:

1. Combine the almond flour with coconut flour then add psyllium husk, xanthan gum, and salt. Mix well.
2. Add egg to the flour mixture then pour coconut oil and almond milk to them mixture.

3. Knead the mixture until it becomes dough then divide the dough into 8.
4. Shape each part of the dough into a donut form then arrange them on a flat surface.
5. Install the crisper plate into the basket of your Power XL then preheat the Power XL for 3 minutes.
6. Select the "Air Fry" menu then set the time to 5 minutes.
7. Arrange the donut in the Power XL's basket then spray olive oil over them.
8. Press the "Start/Stop" button to begin then fry the donuts.
9. Once then Power XL beeps and the donuts are done, remove them from the Power XL, and arrange them on a serving dish. Repeat with the remaining donuts.
10. Once it is done, arrange the donuts on a serving dish and serve.
11. Enjoy it!

Nutrition: 157 Calories, 13.7g Fats, 7.6g Net Carbs, 3.6g Protein

2. Zucchini Strawberry Cheesy Casserole

Preparation Time: 5 Minutes
Cooking Time: 25 Minutes
Servings: 4

Ingredients:

- 2 cups strawberry cubes
- ½ cup zucchini cubes
- ½ cup avocado cubes
- ¼ cup butter, melted
- 2 tablespoons almond flour
- ¼ cup unsweetened almond milk
- 1-cup grated mozzarella cheese

Directions:

1. Prepare a casserole dish that fits the Power XL's basket then coat it with olive oil.
2. Layer avocado cubes, zucchini cubes, and strawberry cubes in the prepared casserole dish then spread evenly.
3. Combine the almond flour with almond milk then stir until incorporated.

4. Add melted butter to the almond milk mixture then mix well.
5. Drizzle the butter mixture over casserole then sprinkle grated mozzarella cheese on top. Set aside.
6. Next, install the crisper plate into the basket of your Power XL then preheat the Power XL for 3 minutes.
7. Select the "Bake" menu then set the temperature to 375°F and adjust the time to 5 minutes.
8. Insert the casserole dish into the Power XL's basket then press the "Start/Stop" button to begin. Bake the casserole.
9. Once the Power XL beeps and the casserole is done, take it out of the Power XL and serve.
10. Enjoy!

Nutrition: 260 Calories, 22.4g Fats, 6.2g Net Carbs, 7.7g Protein

3. Lemon Chili Buttery Baked Pumpkin

Preparation Time: 5 Minutes
Cooking Time: 15 Minutes
Servings: 4

Ingredients:

- 2 cups raw pumpkin
- 1-tablespoon extra-virgin olive oil
- 1-tablespoon lemon juice
- ¼ teaspoon salt
- ¾ teaspoon chili powder
- 2 tablespoons butter

Directions:

1. Cut the pumpkin into medium chunks then place them in a bowl.
2. Drizzle lemon juice and olive oil over then sprinkle salt and chili powder on top. Toss to combine.
3. Next, install the crisper plate into the basket of your Power XL then preheat the Power XL for 3 minutes.

4. Select the "Bake" menu then set the temperature to 375°F and adjust the time to 7 minutes.
5. Spread the seasoned pumpkin in the Power XL's basket then drop butter at several places on the top of the pumpkin.
6. Press the "Start/Stop" button to begin then bake the pumpkin.
7. Once it is done, remove the baked pumpkin from the Power XL and transfer it to a serving dish.
8. Serve and enjoy.

Nutrition: 97 Calories, 9.4g Fats, 3.6g Net Carbs, 0.7g Protein

4. Cabbage Hash Brown with Spinach and Bacon

Preparation Time: 5 Minutes
Cooking Time: 25 Minutes
Servings: 4

Ingredients:

- 2 cups shredded cabbage
- ½ teaspoon garlic salt
- ½ teaspoon pepper
- ¼ teaspoon chili powder
- ½ cup diced onion
- ¼ cup grated cheddar cheese
- 1-cup chopped spinach
- ½ cup chopped bacon
- 2 tablespoons extra virgin olive oil
- 1 egg

Directions:

1. Place the shredded cabbage in a bowl then season it with garlic salt, pepper, and chili powder.
2. Cut the bacon into medium chunks then add it to the shredded cabbage together with diced onion,

cheddar cheese, chopped spinach, olive oil, and egg. Mix well.
3. Next, install the crisper plate and preheat the Power XL for 3 minutes.
4. Select the "Bake" menu then set the temperature to 375°F and set the time to 20 minutes.
5. Transfer the cabbage mixture to the Power XL's basket then spread it evenly.
6. Press the "Start/Stop" button to begin then bake the cabbage mixture.
7. Once the Power XL beeps and the cabbage hash brown is done, take it out and transfer the cabbage hash brown to a serving dish.
8. Serve and enjoy.

Nutrition: 194 Calories, 17.3g Fats, 3.2g Net Carbs, 6.2g Protein

5. Coconut Sandwich with Tomato and Avocado

Preparation Time: 5 Minutes

Cooking Time: 15 Minutes

Servings: 4

Ingredients:

- ½ cup almond flour
- ¼ teaspoon salt
- ¼ teaspoon baking soda
- 2 eggs
- 2 tablespoons coconut oil
- 2 tablespoons coconut milk
- 1 ripe avocado
- 1 large red tomato

Directions:

1. Combine the almond flour with salt and baking soda then mix well.
2. Make a hole in the center of the flour mixture then add eggs, coconut oil, and coconut milk to it. Stir until incorporated.

3. Line a baking pan that fits the Power XL then grease it with cooking spray.
4. Transfer the batter to the prepared baking pan and spread it evenly.
5. Next, install the crisper plate into the basket of your Power XL then preheat the Power XL for 3 minutes.
6. Select the "Bake" menu then set the temperature to 325°F and adjust the time to 10 minutes.
7. Insert the baking pan to the Power XL's basket then press the "Start/Stop" button to begin. Bake the bread.
8. Once the Power XL beeps and the bread is done, remove it from the Power XL and take the bread out of the pan.
9. Cut the bread into thick slices then top each slice of bread with avocado and tomato slices.
10. Serve and enjoy.

Nutrition: 242 Calories, 22.6g Fats, 2.9g Net Carbs, 5g Protein

MAINS: BEEF

1. Easy Beef Roast

Preparation Time: 10 Minutes
Cooking Time: 45 Minutes
Servings: 6

Ingredients:
- 2 ½ lbs. beef roast
- 2 tbsp Italian seasoning

Directions:
1. Arrange roast on the rotisserie spite.
2. Rub roast with Italian seasoning, then insert into the instant vortex air fryer oven.
3. Air fry at 350 F for 45 minutes or until the roast's internal temperature reaches 145 F.
4. Slice and serve.

Nutrition: Calories 365 Fat 13.2 g Carbs 0.5 g Protein 57.4 g

2. Beef Sirloin Roast

Preparation Time: 10 Minutes
Cooking Time: 50 Minutes
Servings: 8

Ingredients:

- 1 tablespoon smoked paprika
- 1 teaspoon ground cumin
- 1 teaspoon garlic powder
- Salt and freshly ground black pepper, to taste
- 2½ pounds sirloin roast

Directions:

1. In a bowl, mix together the spices, salt and black pepper.
2. Rub the roast with spice mixture generously.
3. Place the sirloin roast into the greased baking pan.
4. Press "Power Button" of Power XL Digital Air Fry Oven and turn the dial to select "Air Roast" mode.
5. Press "Time Button" and again turn the dial to set the cooking time to 50 minutes.

6. Now push "Temp Button" and rotate the dial to set the temperature at 350 degrees F.
7. Press "Start/Pause" button to start.
8. When the unit beeps to show that it is preheated, open the lid and insert baking pan in the oven.
9. When cooking time is complete, open the lid and place the roast onto a platter for about 10 minutes before slicing.
10. With a sharp knife, cut the beef roast into desired sized slices and serve.

Nutrition: Calories: 260 Fat: 11.9g Sat Fat: 4.4g Carbohydrates: 0.4g Fiber: 0.1g Sugar: 0.1g Protein: 38g

3. Air Fried Grilled Steak

Preparation Time: 6 Minutes
Cooking Time: 40 Minutes
Servings: 2

Ingredients:

- Two sirloin steaks
- 3 tbsp. butter, melted
- 3 tbsp. olive oil
- Salt and pepper, to taste

Directions:

1. Preheat the Smart Air Fryer Oven for 5 minutes at 350°F.
2. Season the sirloin steaks with olive oil, salt, and pepper.
3. Place the beef in the air fryer basket and put the basket into the oven.
4. Select GRILL. Grill for 40 minutes at 350°F.
5. Once cooked, serve with butter.

Nutrition: Calories 1536 Fat 123.7 g Protein 103.4 g

MAINS: SEAFOOD

1. Lemon-Pepper Tilapia Fillets

Preparation Time: 5 Minutes
Cooking Time: 15 Minutes
Servings: 4

Ingredients:

- Four tilapia fillets
- One teaspoon garlic powder
- One teaspoon paprika
- One teaspoon dried basil
- Lemon-pepper seasoning, to taste

Directions:

1. Heat the air fryer to 400°F (205°C).
2. Add the olive oil, garlic powder, paprika, basil, lemon-pepper seasoning, fillets to a large bowl, and toss well to coat the fillets thoroughly.
3. Transfer the coated fillets to the air fryer basket.

4. Cook in the warmed air fryer for 8 minutes. Flip the fillets and cook for 7 minutes more until the fish flakes easily with a fork.
5. Divide the fillets among four serving plates and serve hot.

Nutrition: Calories: 131 Fat: 3.6g Carbs: 1.1g Protein: 23.6g

2. Blackened Shrimp with Lemon Juice

Preparation Time: 5 Minutes
Cooking Time: 10 Minutes
Servings: 4

Ingredients:

- 1 pound (454 g) raw shrimp, peeled, deveined, and patted dry
- One teaspoon paprika
- ½ teaspoon cayenne pepper
- ½ teaspoon dried oregano
- Juice of ½ lemon

Directions:

1. Heat the air fryer to 400°F (205°C).
2. Put the shrimp in a sealable plastic bag. Add the paprika, cayenne pepper, oregano, lemon juice, salt, and pepper to the shrimp. Lid the bag and shake to coat the shrimp with the spices evenly.

3. Spray the air fryer basket with cooking spray. Arrange the shrimp in the basket.
4. Cook in the warmed air fryer for 7 minutes, shaking the basket once during cooking, or until the shrimp is blackened.
5. Let the shrimp cool for 5 minutes and serve warm.

Nutrition: Calories: 102 Fat: 2.1g Carbs: 0g Protein: 21.1g

3. Fried Catfish with Fish Fry

Preparation Time: 5 Minutes

Cooking Time: 13 Minutes

Servings: 4

Ingredients:

- Four catfish fillets rinsed and patted dry
- ¼ cup seasoned fish fry
- One tablespoon chopped parsley
- One tablespoon olive oil

Directions:

1. Warm the air fryer to 400°F (205°C).
2. Put the fillets and seasoned fish fry in a Ziploc bag. Cover the bag and shake well until the fish is nicely coated.
3. Brush both sides of each piece of fish with olive oil. Put the fillets in the air fryer basket.
4. Cook in the preheated air fryer for 13 minutes. Flip the fillets once during cooking or until the fish is cooked through.
5. Remove from the basket and garnish with chopped parsley.

Nutrition: Calories: 209 Fat: 5.2g Carbs: 8.1g Protein: 17.1g

4. Pecan-Crusted Catfish Fillets

Preparation Time: 5 Minutes
Cooking Time: 12 Minutes
Servings: 4

Ingredients:

- ½ cup pecan meal
- 4 (4-ounce / 113-g) catfish fillets, rinsed and patted dry
- Fresh oregano, for garnish (optional)
- Pecan halves, for garnish (optional)

Directions:

1. Warm the air fryer to 375°F (190°C). Grease the air fryer basket with half of the avocado oil and set aside.
2. Stir together the pecan meal, salt, and pepper in a large bowl. Roll the fillets with the mixture, pressing, so the fish is well coated.
3. Brush the fillets with the remaining avocado oil and transfer to the air fryer basket.

4. Cook in the preheated air fryer for 12 minutes, flipping the fillets halfway through, or until the fish flakes easily with a fork.
5. Remove from the basket to a large plate. Sprinkle the oregano and pecan halves on top for garnish, if desired.

Nutrition: Calories: 163 Fat: 11.1g Carbs: 1.2g Protein: 17.2g

5. Fish Fillets with Parmesan Cheese

Preparation Time: 5 Minutes
Cooking Time: 10 to 12 Minutes
Servings: 4

Ingredients:

- 1 cup Parmesan cheese, grated
- One egg whisked
- One teaspoon garlic powder
- ½ teaspoon shallot powder
- Four white fish fillets

Directions:

1. Preheat the air fryer to 370°F (188°C).
2. In a shallow dish, put the Parmesan cheese. Mix the whisked egg, garlic powder, and shallot powder in a bowl, and stir to combine.
3. On a clean surface, season the fillets generously with salt and pepper. Dredge the fillets into the

egg mixture, then roll over the cheese until thickly coated.
4. Assemble the fillets in the air fryer basket and air fry until golden brown, about 10 to 12 minutes.
5. Let the fish fillets cool for 5 minutes before serving.

Nutrition: Calories: 298 Fat: 7.8g Carbs: 5.5g Protein: 0.9g

6. Air-Fried Sardines

Preparation Time: 10 Minutes
Cooking Time: 12 Minutes
Servings: 4

Ingredients:

- 1½ pounds (680 g) sardines, rinsed and patted dry
- One tablespoon lemon juice
- One tablespoon Italian seasoning mix

Directions:

1. Warm the air fryer to 350°F (180°C).
2. In a large bowl, toss the sardines with olive oil, lemon juice, Italian seasoning mix, soy sauce, salt, and pepper. Let the sardines marinate for 30 minutes.
3. Put the marinated sardines in the air fryer basket and air fry for about 12 minutes until flaky, flipping the fish halfway through.
4. Transfer to a plate and serve hot.

Nutrition: Calories: 438 Fat: 26.3g Carbs: 3.6g Protein: 42.6g

MAINS: VEGETABLES

1. Curried Eggplant Slices

Preparation Time: 10 Minutes
Cooking Time: 10 Minutes
Servings: 2

Ingredients:

- 1 large eggplant
- 1 garlic clove, minced
- 1 tbsp olive oil
- 1/2 tsp curry powder
- 1/8 tsp turmeric
- Salt

Directions:

1. Preheat the air fryer to 300 F.
2. Add all fixings into the large mixing bowl then toss to coat.
3. Transfer eggplant slices into the air fryer basket.
4. Cook eggplant slices for 10 minutes or until lightly brown. Shake basket halfway through.
5. Serve and enjoy.

Nutrition: Calories 122 Fat 7.5 g Carbohydrates 14.4 g Sugar 6.9 g Protein 2.4 g Cholesterol 0 mg

2. Healthy Green Beans

Preparation Time: 5 Minutes
Cooking Time: 6 Minutes
Servings: 4

Ingredients:

- 1 lb. green beans, trimmed
- Pepper
- Salt

Directions:

1. Spray air fryer basket with cooking spray.
2. Preheat the air fryer to 400 F.
3. Add green beans in air fryer basket and season with pepper and salt.
4. Cook green beans for 6 minutes. Turn halfway through.
5. Serve and enjoy.

Nutrition: Calories 35 Fat 0.1 g Carbohydrates 8.1 g Sugar 1.6 g Protein 2.1 g Cholesterol 0 mg

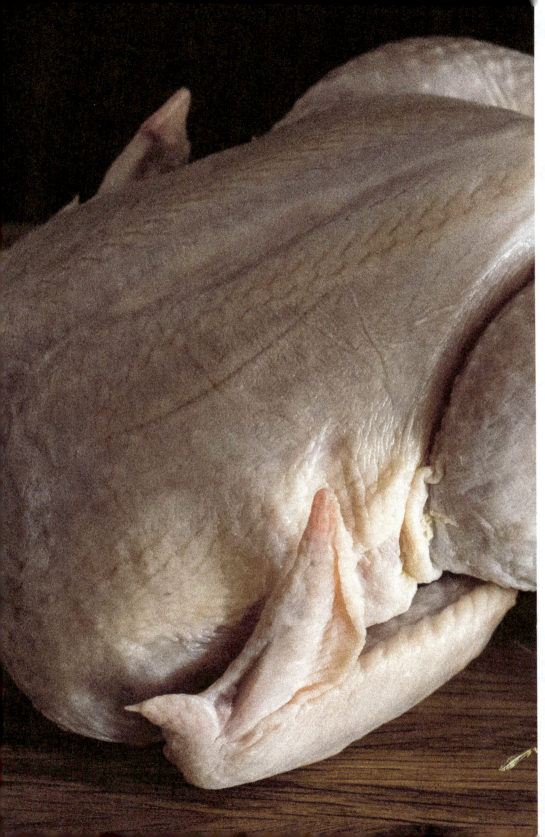

MAINS: POULTRY

1. Spicy Air-Crisped Chicken and Potatoes

Preparation Time: 5 Minutes
Cooking Time: 25 Minutes
Servings: 4

Ingredients:
- 4 bone-in, skin-on chicken thighs
- ½ teaspoon kosher salt or ¼ teaspoon fine salt
- 2 tablespoons melted unsalted butter
- 2 teaspoons Worcestershire sauce
- 2 teaspoons curry powder
- 1 teaspoon dried oregano leaves
- ½ teaspoon dry mustard
- ½ teaspoon granulated garlic
- ¼ teaspoon paprika
- ¼ teaspoon hot pepper sauce, such as Tabasco
- Cooking oil spray
- 4 medium Yukon gold potatoes, chopped
- 1 tablespoon extra-virgin olive oil

Directions:
1. Sprinkle the chicken thighs on both sides with salt.
2. In a medium bowl, stir together the melted butter, Worcestershire sauce, curry powder, oregano, dry mustard, granulated garlic, paprika, and hot pepper sauce. Add the thighs to the sauce and stir to coat.
3. Insert the crisper plate into the basket and the basket into the unit. Preheat the unit by selecting AIR FRY, setting the temperature to 400°F, and setting the time to 3 minutes. Select START/STOP to begin.
4. Once the unit is preheated, spray the crisper plate with cooking oil. In the basket, combine the potatoes and olive oil and toss to coat.
5. Add the wire rack to the air fryer and place the chicken thighs on top.
6. Select AIR FRY, set the temperature to 400°F, and set the time to 25 minutes. Select START/STOP to begin.
7. After 19 minutes check the chicken thighs. If a food thermometer inserted into the chicken registers 165°F, transfer them to a clean plate, and cover with aluminum foil to keep warm. If they aren't cooked to 165°F, resume cooking for another 1 to 2 minutes until they are done. Remove them from the unit along with the rack.

8. Remove the basket and shake it to distribute the potatoes. Reinsert the basket to resume cooking for 3 to 6 minutes, or until the potatoes are crisp and golden brown.
9. When the cooking is complete, serve the chicken with the potatoes.

Nutrition: Calories: 333; Total fat: 14g; Saturated fat: 5g; Cholesterol: 109mg; Sodium: 428mg; Carbohydrates: 27g; Fiber: 3g; Protein: 25g

2. Buttermilk Fried Chicken

Preparation Time: 7 Minutes
Cooking Time: 20 to 25 Minutes
Servings: 4

Ingredients:

- 1 cup all-purpose flour
- 2 teaspoons paprika
- Pinch salt
- Freshly ground black pepper
- 1/3 cup buttermilk
- 2 eggs
- 2 tablespoons extra-virgin olive oil
- 1½ cups bread crumbs
- 6 chicken pieces, drumsticks, breasts, and thighs, patted dry
- Cooking oil spray

Directions:

1. In a shallow bowl, stir together the flour, paprika, salt, and pepper.
2. In another bowl, beat the buttermilk and eggs until smooth.

3. In a third bowl, stir together the olive oil and bread crumbs until mixed.
4. Dredge the chicken in the flour, dip in the eggs to coat, and finally press into the bread crumbs, patting the crumbs firmly onto the chicken skin.
5. Insert the crisper plate into the basket and the basket into the unit. Preheat the unit by selecting AIR FRY, setting the temperature to 375°F, and setting the time to 3 minutes. Select START/STOP to begin.
6. Once the unit is preheated, spray the crisper plate with cooking oil. Place the chicken into the basket.
7. Select AIR FRY, set the temperature to 375°F, and set the time to 25 minutes. Select START/STOP to begin.
8. After 10 minutes, flip the chicken. Resume cooking. After 10 minutes more, check the chicken. If a food thermometer inserted into the chicken registers 165°F and the chicken is brown and crisp, it is done. Otherwise, resume cooking for up to 5 minutes longer.
9. When the cooking is complete, let cool for 5 minutes, then serve.

Nutrition: Calories: 644; Total fat: 17g; Saturated fat: 4g; Cholesterol: 214mg; Sodium: 495mg; Carbohydrates: 55g; Fiber: 3g; Protein: 62g

3. Korean Chicken Wings

Preparation Time: 10 Minutes
Cooking Time: 25 Minutes
Servings: 4

Ingredients:

- ¼ cup gochujang, or red pepper paste
- ¼ cup mayonnaise
- 2 tablespoons honey
- 1 tablespoon sesame oil
- 2 teaspoons minced garlic
- 1 tablespoon sugar
- 2 teaspoons ground ginger
- 3 pounds whole chicken wings
- Olive oil spray
- 1 teaspoon salt
- ½ teaspoon freshly ground black pepper

Directions:

1. In a large bowl, whisk the gochujang, mayonnaise, honey, sesame oil, garlic, sugar, and ginger. Set aside.
2. Insert the crisper plate into the basket and the basket into the unit. Preheat the unit by selecting AIR FRY, setting the temperature to 400°F, and setting the time to 3 minutes. Select START/STOP to begin.
3. To prepare the chicken wings, cut the wings in half. The meatier part is the drumette. Cut off and discard the wing tip from the flat part (or save the wing tips in the freezer to make chicken stock).
4. Once the unit is preheated, spray the crisper plate with olive oil. Working in batches, place half the chicken wings into the basket, spray them with olive oil, and sprinkle with the salt and pepper.
5. Select AIR FRY, set the temperature to 400°F, and set the time to 20 minutes. Select START/STOP to begin.
6. After 10 minutes, remove the basket, flip the wings, and spray them with more olive oil. Reinsert the basket to resume cooking.
7. Cook the wings to an internal temperature of 165°F, then transfer them to the bowl with the prepared sauce and toss to coat.

8. Repeat steps 4, 5, 6, and 7 for the remaining chicken wings.
9. Return the coated wings to the basket and air fry for 4 to 6 minutes more until the sauce has glazed the wings and the chicken is crisp. After 3 minutes, check the wings to make sure they aren't burning. Serve hot.

Nutrition: Calories: 913; Total fat: 66g; Saturated fat: 15g; Cholesterol: 244mg; Sodium: 1,722mg; Carbohydrates: 23g; Fiber: 1g; Protein: 59g

4. Paprika Chicken Wings

Preparation Time: 15 Minutes
Cooking Time: 24 Minutes
Servings: 6

Ingredients:

- 1 ½ lb. chicken wings
- 1/4 teaspoon sea salt
- 1/2 teaspoon black pepper
- 1/2 teaspoon smoked paprika
- 1/2 teaspoon garlic powder

Directions:

1. Mix smoked paprika, black pepper, salt, garlic powder, baking powder, and onion powder in a small bowl.
2. Add all the chicken wings to a large bowl and drizzle the spice mixture over the wings.
3. Toss well and transfer the wings to an Air Fryer basket.
4. Return the Air Fryer basket to the Air Fryer.

5. Select the Air Fry mode at 400 degrees F for 24 minutes.
6. Toss the wings once cooked halfway through.
7. Serve warm.

Nutrition: Calories 220 Fat 1.7g Sodium 178mg Carbs 1.7g Fiber 0.2g Sugar 0.2g Protein 32.9g

MAINS: PORK

1. Spiced Pork Shoulder

Preparation Time: 15 Minutes
Cooking Time: 55 Minutes
Servings: 6

Ingredients:

- One teaspoon ground cumin
- One teaspoon cayenne pepper
- One teaspoon garlic powder
- Salt and ground black pepper, as required
- 2 pounds skin-on pork shoulder

Directions:

1. In a small container, mix the spices, salt, and black pepper.
2. Arrange the pork shoulder onto a cutting board, skin-side down.
3. Season the inner side of pork shoulder with salt and black pepper.
4. With kitchen twines, tie the pork shoulder into a long round cylinder shape.
5. Season the outer side of pork shoulder with spice mixture.

6. Insert the rotisserie rod through the pork shoulder.
7. Insert the rotisserie forks, one on each hand of the rod to secure the pork shoulder.
8. Select "Roast" and then adjust the temperature to 350 degrees F.
9. Set the timer for 55 minutes and press the "Start."
10. When the display shows "Add Food," press the red lever down.
11. Weight the left side of the rod into the Vortex.
12. Change the rod's left side into the groove lengthways, the metal bar, so it doesn't move.
13. Then, close the door and touch "Rotate."
14. Press the red lever to release the rod when cooking time is complete.
15. Remove the pork from Spiral and place onto a platter for about 10 minutes before slicing.
16. By a sharp knife, cut the pork shoulder into desired sized slices and serve.

Nutrition: Calories 445 Fat 32.5 g Carbs 0.7 g Protein 35.4 g

2. Seasoned Pork Tenderloin

Preparation Time: 10 Minutes
Cooking Time: 45 Minutes
Servings: 5

Ingredients:

- 1½ pounds pork tenderloin
- 2-3 tablespoons BBQ pork seasoning

Directions:

1. Rub the pork with seasoning generously. Insert the rotisserie rod through the pork tenderloin.
2. Pull-out the rotisserie forks, one on each side of the rod, to secure the pork tenderloin.
3. Select "Roast" and then adjust the temperature to 360 degrees F.
4. Set the timer for 45 minutes and press the "Start."
5. When the display shows "Add Food," press the red lever down.
6. Weight the left side of the rod into the Vortex.
7. Now, change the rod's left side into the groove in line with the metal bar, so it doesn't move.
8. Then, close the door and touch "Rotate."

9. Press the red lever to release the rod when cooking time is complete.
10. Remove the pork from Vortex and place it onto a platter for about 10 minutes before slicing.
11. With a sharp knife, cut the roast into desired sized slices and serve.

Nutrition: Calories 195 Fat 4.8 g Carbs 0 g Protein 35.6 g

3. Garlicky Pork Tenderloin

Preparation Time: 15 Minutes
Cooking Time: 20 Minutes
Servings: 5

Ingredients:

- 1½ pounds pork tenderloin
- Nonstick cooking spray
- Two small heads of roasted garlic
- Salt and ground black pepper, as required

Directions:

1. Lightly spray all the pork sides with cooking spray and then season with salt and black pepper.
2. Now, rub the pork with roasted garlic. Arrange the roast onto the lightly greased cooking tray.
3. Select "Air Fry" and then regulate the temperature to 400 degrees F. Set the timer for 20 minutes and press the "Start."
4. When the display demonstrates "Add Food," insert the cooking tray in the center position.
5. If the display shows "Turn Food," turn the pork.

6. When cooking time is done, remove the tray from Vortex.
7. Place the roast onto a platter for about 10 minutes before slicing.
8. With a sharp knife, cut the roast into desired sized slices and serve.

Nutrition: Calories 202 Fat 4.8 g Carbs 1.7 g Protein 35.9 g

SNACKS

1. Personal Mozzarella Pizza Crust

Preparation Time: 5 Minutes
Cooking Time: 10 Minutes
Servings: 1

Ingredients:

- ½ cup shredded whole-milk mozzarella cheese
- Two tablespoons blanched finely ground almond flour
- One tablespoon full-fat cream cheese
- One large egg white

Directions:

1. Place mozzarella, almond flour, and cream cheese in a medium microwave-safe bowl. Microwave for 30 seconds. Stir until an even ball of dough is made. Add egg white, then stirring until soft round dough forms.
2. Press into a 6" round pizza crust.
3. Cut a piece of parchment to suit your air fryer basket and place crust on parchment.

4. Regulate the temperature to 350°F and set the timer for 10 minutes.
5. Flip after 5 minutes. During this time, put any desired toppings on the crust. Continue cooking until golden. Serve immediately.

Nutrition: Calories: 314 Protein: 19.9 g Fiber: 1.5 g Net carbohydrates: *3.6 g* Fat: 22.7 g Sodium: 457 mg Carbohydrates: 5.1 g Sugar: 1.8 g

2. Garlic Cheese Bread

Preparation Time: 10 Minutes
Cooking Time: 10 Minutes
Servings: 2

Ingredients:

- 1 cup shredded mozzarella cheese
- ¼ cup grated Parmesan cheese
- One large egg
- ½ teaspoon garlic powder

Directions:

1. Mix all fixings in a large bowl. Torn a piece of parchment to fit your air fryer basket. Press the mixture into a circle on the parchment and place it into the air fryer basket.
2. Regulate the temperature to 350°F and set the timer for 10 minutes.
3. Serve warm.

Nutrition: Calories: 258 Protein: 19.2 g Fiber: 0.1 g Net carbohydrates: 3.6 g Fat: 16.6 g Sodium: 612 mg Carbohydrates: 3.7 g Sugar: 0.7 g

3. Crustless Three-Meat Pizza

Preparation Time: 5 Minutes
Cooking Time: 5 Minutes
Servings: 1
Ingredients:

- ½ cup shredded mozzarella cheese
- Seven slices pepperoni
- ¼ cup cooked ground sausage
- Two slices sugar-free bacon, cooked and crumbled
- One tablespoon grated Parmesan cheese

Directions:

1. Cover the bottom of a 6" cake pan with mozzarella. Place pepperoni, sausage, and bacon on top of the cheese and sprinkle with Parmesan. Place pan into the air fryer basket.
2. Regulate the temperature to 400°F and set the timer for 5 minutes.
3. Remove when the cheese is bubbling and golden. Serve warm with pizza sauce for dipping.

Nutrition: Calories: 466 Protein: 28.1 g Fiber: 0.5 g Net carbohydrates: 4.7 g Fat: 34.0 g Sodium: 1,446 mg Carbohydrates: 5.2 g Sugar: 1.6 g

4. Bacon-Wrapped Brie

Preparation Time: 5 Minutes
Cooking Time: 10 Minutes
Servings: 8

Ingredients:

- Four slices of sugar-free bacon
- 1 (8-ounce) round Brie

Directions:

1. Put two slices of bacon to form an X. Then place the third slice of bacon parallel across the center of the X. Place the fourth slice of bacon straight up across the X. Then it should look like a plus sign (+) on top of an X. Position the Brie in the middle of the bacon.
2. Wrap the bacon around the Brie, locking with a few toothpicks. Torn a piece of parchment to fit your air fryer basket and place the bacon-wrapped Brie on top. Put it inside the basket of the air fryer.
3. Alter the temperature to 400°F, then change the timer for 10 minutes.

4. When 3 minutes keep on on the timer, cautiously flip Brie.
5. When cooked, bacon will be crunchy, and cheese will be soft and melty. When serving it, cut into eight slices.

Nutrition: Calories: 116 Protein: 7.7 g Fiber: 0.0 g Net carbohydrates: *0.2 g* Fat: 8.9 g Sodium: 259 mg Carbohydrates: 0.2 g Sugar: 0.1 g

5. Smoky BBQ Roasted Almonds

Preparation Time: 5 Minutes

Cooking Time: 6 Minutes

Servings: 4

Ingredients:

- 1 cup of raw almonds
- Two teaspoons coconut oil
- One teaspoon chili powder
- ¼ teaspoon cumin
- ¼ teaspoon smoked paprika

Directions:

1. In a large bowl, toss all fixings until almonds are evenly coated with oil and spices. Place almonds into the air fryer basket.
2. Regulate the temperature to 320°F and set the timer for 6 minutes.
3. Toss the fryer basket midway through the cooking time.
4. Allow cooling completely.

Nutrition: Calories: 182 Protein: 6.2 g Fiber: 3.3 g Net carbohydrates: 3.3 g Fat: 16.3 g

Sodium: 19 mg Carbohydrates: 6.6 g Sugar: 1.1 g

SIDES

1. Low-Calorie Beets Dish

Preparation Time: 10 Minutes
Cooking Time: 10 Minutes
Servings: 2

Ingredients:

- Four whole beets
- One tablespoon balsamic vinegar
- One tablespoon olive oil
- Salt and pepper to taste
- Two springs rosemary

Directions:

1. Wash your beets and peel them
2. Cut beets into cubes
3. Take a bowl and mix in rosemary, pepper, salt, vinegar
4. Cover beets with the prepared sauce

5. Coat the beets with olive oil
6. Pre-heat your Fryer to 400-degree F
7. Transfer beets to Air Fryer cooking basket and cook for 10 minutes
8. Serve with your cheese sauce and enjoy!

Nutrition: Calories: 149 Fat: 1g Carbohydrates: 5g Protein: 30g

2. Broccoli and Parmesan Dish

Preparation Time: 5 Minutes
Cooking Time: 20 Minutes
Servings: 4

Ingredients:

- One fresh head broccoli
- One tablespoon olive oil
- One lemon, juiced
- Salt and pepper to taste
- 1-ounce parmesan cheese, grated

Directions:

1. Wash broccoli thoroughly and cut them into florets.
2. Add the listed ingredients to your broccoli and mix well.
3. Preheat your fryer to 365-degree F.
4. Air fry broccoli for 20 minutes.
5. Serve and enjoy!

Nutrition: Calories: 114 Fat: 6g Carbohydrates: 10 g Protein: 7g

3. Bacon and Asparagus Spears

Preparation Time: 15 Minutes

Cooking Time: 8 Minutes

Servings: 4

Ingredients:

- 20 spears asparagus
- Four bacon slices
- One tablespoon olive oil
- One tablespoon sesame oil
- One garlic clove, crushed

Directions:

1. Warm your Air Fryer to 380 degrees F
2. Take a small bowl and add oil, crushed garlic, and mix
3. Separate asparagus into four bunches and wrap them in bacon

4. Brush wraps with oil and garlic mix, transfer to your Air Fryer basket
5. Cook for 8 minutes
6. Serve and enjoy!

Nutrition: Calories: 175 Fat: 15g Carbohydrates: 6g Protein: 5g

4. Healthy Low Carb Fish Nugget

Preparation Time: 5 Minutes

Cooking Time: 10 Minutes

Servings: 4

Ingredients:

- 1-pound fresh cod
- Two tablespoons olive oil
- ½ cup almond flour
- Two larges finely beaten eggs
- 1-2 cups almond meal

Directions:

1. Preheat your Air Fryer to 388 degrees F
2. Take a food processor and add olive oil, almond meal, salt, and blend
3. Take three bowls and add almond flour, almond meal, beaten eggs individually
4. Take cods and cut them into slices of 1-inch thickness and 2-inch length
5. Dredge slices into flour, eggs, and crumbs
6. Transfer nuggets to Air Fryer cooking basket and cook for 10 minutes until golden
7. Serve and enjoy!

Nutrition: Calories: 196 Fat: 14g Carbohydrates: 6g Protein: 14g

5. Fried Up Pumpkin Seeds

Preparation Time: 10 Minutes
Cooking Time: 60 Minutes
Servings: 2

Ingredients:

- One and ½ cups pumpkin seeds
- Olive oil as needed
- One and ½ teaspoons salt
- One teaspoon smoked paprika

Directions:

1. Cut pumpkin and scrape out seeds and flesh
2. Separate flesh from seeds and rinse the seeds under cold water
3. Bring two-quarter of salted water to boil and add seeds, boil for 10 minutes
4. Drain seeds and spread them on a kitchen towel
5. Dry for 20 minutes

6. Preheat your fryer to 350 degrees F
7. Take a bowl and add seeds, smoked paprika, and olive oil
8. Season with salt and transfer to your Air Fryer cooking basket
9. Cook for 35 minutes, enjoy it!

Nutrition: Calories: 237 Fat: 21g Carbohydrates: 4g Protein: 12g

6. Decisive Tiger Shrimp Platter

Preparation Time: 5 Minutes
Cooking Time: 10 Minutes
Servings: 6

Ingredients:

- One ¼ pound tiger shrimp, or a count of about 16 to 20
- ¼ teaspoons cayenne pepper
- ½ teaspoons old bay seasoning
- ¼ teaspoons smoked paprika
- One tablespoon olive oil

Directions:

1. Pre-heat your Fryer to 390-degree Fahrenheit
2. Take a bowl and add the listed ingredients
3. Mix well
4. Transfer the shrimp to your fryer cooking basket and cook for 5 minutes
5. Remove and serve the shrimp over cauliflower rice if preferred
6. Enjoy!

Nutrition: Calories: 251 Carbohydrate: 3g Protein: 17g Fat: 19g

DESSERT

1. Vegan Donuts

Preparation Time: 10 Minutes
Cooking Time: 15 Minutes
Servings: 4
Ingredients:

- 8 ounces whole wheat flour
- Two tablespoons coconut sugar
- One tablespoon flax meal mixed with two tablespoons water
- Two and ½ tablespoons vegetable oil
- One teaspoon baking powder

Directions:

1. In a bowl, mix one tablespoon oil with sugar, baking powder, and flour and stir.
2. In a second bowl, mix the flax meal with one and ½ tablespoons oil and milk and stir well.
3. Combine the two mixtures, stir, shape donuts from this mix, place them in your air fryer's basket and cook using 360 degrees F for 15 minutes.
4. Serve them warm.
5. Enjoy!

Nutrition: Calories 210 Fat 12 Fiber 1 Carbs 12 Protein 4

2. Cinnamon Rice with Coconut

Preparation Time: 10 Minutes
Cooking Time: 35 Minutes
Servings: 4

Ingredients:

- Three and ½ cups of water
- 1 cup of coconut sugar
- 2 cups white rice, washed and rinsed
- Two cinnamon sticks
- ½ cup coconut, shredded

Directions:

1. In your air fryer, mix water with coconut sugar, rice, cinnamon, and coconut, stir, cover, and cook at 365 degrees F for 35 minutes.
2. Divide pudding into cups and serve cold.
3. Enjoy!

Nutrition: Calories 213 Fat 4 Fiber 6 Carbs 9 Protein 4

3. Pineapple and Apricots

Preparation Time: 10 Minutes
Cooking Time: 12 Minutes
Servings: 10

Ingredients:

- 6 cups canned pineapple chunks, drained
- 4 cups canned apricots, halved and drained
- 3 cups natural applesauce
- 2 cups canned mandarin oranges, drained
- Two tablespoons stevia

Directions:

1. Put pineapples, apricots, applesauce, oranges, cinnamon, and stevia in a pan that fits your air fryer, introduce in the fryer, and cook at 360 degrees F for 12 minutes.
2. Divide into small bowls and serve cold.
3. Enjoy!

4. Air-Fried Smores

Preparation Time: 5 Minutes
Cooking Time: 5 Minutes
Servings: 4

Ingredients:

- Whole graham crackers (4)
- Marshmallows (2)
- Chocolate - such as Hershey's (4 pieces)

Directions:

1. Tear the graham crackers in half to make eight squares. Cut the marshmallows in half crosswise with a pair of scissors.
2. Place the marshmallows cut side down on four graham squares. Place marshmallow side up in the Air Fryer basket, cook at 390° Fahrenheit for four to five minutes or wait until golden.

3. Remove them from the fryer and place a piece Break all graham crackers in half to create eight squares—cut marshmallows in half crosswise with a pair of scissors.
4. Place the marshmallows, cut side down, on four graham squares of chocolate and graham square on top of each toasted marshmallow and serve.

Nutrition: Calories: 540 Fat: 6.2g Carbs: 96.0g Protein: 29.6g

5. Banana Smores

Preparation Time: 5 Minutes
Cooking Time: 5 Minutes
Servings: 4

Ingredients:

- Bananas (4)
- Mini-peanut butter chips (3 tbsp.)
- Graham cracker cereal (3 tbsp.)
- Mini-chocolate chips - semi-sweet (3 tbsp.)

Directions:

1. Heat the Air Fryer in advance at 400° Fahrenheit.
2. Slice the un-peeled bananas lengthwise along the inside of the curve. Don't slice through the bottom of the peel. Open slightly - forming a pocket.
3. Fill each pocket with chocolate chips, peanut butter chips, and marshmallows. Poke the cereal into the filling.

4. Arrange the stuffed bananas in the fryer basket, keeping them upright with the filling facing up.
5. Air-fry until the peel has blackened and the chocolate and marshmallows have toasted (6 minutes).
6. Chill for 1-2 minutes. Spoon out the filling to serve.

Nutrition: Calories: 540 Fat: 6.2g Carbs: 96.0g Protein: 29.6g

6. Cherry Pie

Preparation Time: 5 Minutes
Cooking Time: 25 Minutes
Servings: 8

Ingredients:

- Cherry pie filling (21 oz. can)
- Milk (1 tbsp.)
- Refrigerated pie crusts (2)
- Egg yolk (1)

Directions:
1. Warm the fryer at 310° Fahrenheit.
2. Poke holes into the crust after placing it on a pie plate. Allow the excess to hang over the edges. Place in the Air Fryer for five (5) minutes
3. Transfer the basket with the pie plate onto the countertop.
4. Fill it with the cherries. Remove the excess crust.
5. Cut the remaining crust into ¾-inch strips - weaving a lattice across the pie.

6. Make an egg wash using the milk and egg. Brush the pie—Air-fry for 15 minutes. Serve with a scoop of ice cream.

Nutrition: Calories 205 Fat 34 Fiber 2 Carbs 6 Protein 2

CONCLUSION

I'm glad you made it this far.

This cookbook is great for everyone and will make you a real chef!

Eating healthy is very important and thanks to these recipes you can do it without giving up the incredible flavor of each food. I hope that creating healthy and tasty dishes has been really fun for you but above all I hope you have recreated each recipe in the best possible way and that you enjoyed doing it!

With this recipe book, it is almost impossible to create dishes that do not match the Air Fryer Power XL!

Now the next step is to keep practicing until you become a real master of the kitchen with the Air fryer Power XL!

Good luck!

CPSIA information can be obtained
at www.ICGtesting.com
Printed in the USA
LVHW021359250421
685423LV00002B/56